The
United Nations

Global Leadership

Decolonization: Dismantling
Empires and Building Independence

The Five Permanent Members of the Security Council:
Responsibilities and Roles

The History and Structure of the United Nations:
Development and Function

Humanitarian Relief Operations:
Lending a Helping Hand

International Security: Peacekeeping and
Peace-Building Around the World

Pioneering International Law:
Conventions, Treaties, and Standards

UN Action Against Terrorism: Fighting Fear

The UN and Cultural Globalization:
One World, Many People

The UN and the Global Marketplace:
Economic Developments

UNICEF and Other Human Rights Efforts:
Protecting Individuals

The UN and the Global Marketplace

Economic Developments

by Heather Docalavich

Mason Crest Publishers

Philadelphia

Mason Crest Publishers Inc.
370 Reed Road
Broomall, Pennsylvania 19008
(866) MCP-BOOK (toll free)

First printing
1 2 3 4 5 6 7 8 9 10

Library of Congress Cataloging-in-Publication Data

Docalavich, Heather.
  The UN and the global marketplace : economic developments / by Heather Docalavich.
      p. cm. — (The United Nations—global leadership)
  Includes bibliographical references and index.
  ISBN 1-4222-0074-4 ISBN 1-4222-0065-5 (series)
  1. United Nations. 2. Economic development. 3. Sustainable development. I. Title: United Nations and the global marketplace. II. Title. III. Series.
  JZ4972.D63 2007
  338.91—dc22
                              2006001492

Interior design by Benjamin Stewart.
Interiors produced by Harding House Publishing Service, Inc.
www.hardinghousepages.com
Cover design by Peter Culatta.
Printed in the Hashemite Kingdom of Jordan.

Contents

Introduction 6

1. Economic Development 9

2. Sustainable Development 21

3. Agenda 21 43

4. Development Programs 53

5. Financing Development 65

Time Line 76

Glossary 77

Further Reading 79

For More Information 80

Reports and Projects 82

Bibliography 84

Index 85

Picture Credits 87

Biographies 88

Introduction
by Dr. Bruce Russett

The United Nations was founded in 1945 by the victors of World War II. They hoped the new organization could learn from the mistakes of the League of Nations that followed World War I—and prevent another war.

The United Nations has not been able to bring worldwide peace; that would be an unrealistic hope. But it has contributed in important ways to the world's experience of more than sixty years without a new world war. Despite its flaws, the United Nations has contributed to peace.

Like any big organization, the United Nations is composed of many separate units with different jobs. These units make three different kinds of contributions. The most obvious to students in North America and other democracies are those that can have a direct and immediate impact for peace.

Especially prominent is the Security Council, which is the only UN unit that can authorize the use of military force against countries and can require all UN members to cooperate in isolating an aggressor country's economy. In the Security Council, each of the big powers—Britain, China, France, Russia, and the United States—can veto any proposed action. That's because the founders of United Nations recognized that if the Council tried to take any military action against the strong opposition of a big power it would result in war. As a result, the United Nations was often sidelined during the Cold War era. Since the end of the Cold War in 1990, however, the Council has authorized many military actions, some directed against specific aggressors but most intended as more neutral peacekeeping efforts. Most of its peacekeeping efforts have been to end civil wars rather than wars between countries. Not all have succeeded, but many have. The United Nations Secretary-General also has had an important role in mediating some conflicts.

UN units that promote trade and economic development make a different kind of contribution. Some help to establish free markets for greater prosperity, or like the UN Development Programme, provide economic and technical assistance to reduce poverty in poor countries. Some are especially concerned with environmental problems or health issues. For example, the World Health Organization and UNICEF deserve great credit for eliminating the deadly disease of smallpox from the world. Poor countries especially support the United Nations for this reason. Since many wars, within and between countries, stem from economic deprivation, these efforts make an important indirect contribution to peace.

Still other units make a third contribution: they promote human rights. The High Commission for Refugees, for example, has worked to ease the distress of millions of refugees who have fled their countries to escape from war and political persecution. A special unit of the Secretary-General's office has supervised and assisted free elections in more than ninety countries. It tries to establish stable and democratic governments in newly independent countries or in countries where the people have defeated a dictatorial government. Other units promote the rights of women, children, and religious and ethnic minorities. The General Assembly provides a useful setting for debate on these and other issues.

These three kinds of action—to end violence, to reduce poverty, and to promote social and political justice—all make a contribution to peace. True peace requires all three, working together.

The UN does not always succeed: like individuals, it makes mistakes . . . and it often learns from its mistakes. Despite the United Nations' occasional stumbles, over the years it has grown and moved forward. These books will show you how.

The UN building in New York City

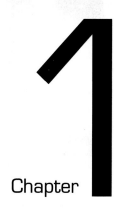

Chapter **1**

Economic Development

The basic purpose of development is to enlarge people's choices. In principle, these choices can be infinite and can change over time. People often value achievements that do not show up at all, or not immediately, in income or growth figures: greater access to knowledge, better nutrition and health services, more secure livelihoods, security against crime and physical violence, satisfying leisure hours, political and cultural freedoms and sense of participation in community activities. The objective of development is to create an enabling environment for people to enjoy long, healthy and creative lives.

—Mahbub ul Haq

The UN and the Global Marketplace: Economic Developments

At the United Nations Millennium Summit in September 2000, world leaders agreed to a new set of global development goals. Designed to combat poverty, hunger, disease, illiteracy, environmental damage, and discrimination against women, these Millennium Development Goals address not only human development but provide a framework for the UN's economic development efforts. The eight Millennium Development Goals were designed to be both measurable and achievable.

1. Eradicate extreme poverty and hunger.
2. Achieve universal primary education.
3. Promote gender equality and empower women.
4. Reduce child mortality.
5. Improve maternal health.
6. Combat HIV/AIDS, malaria, and other diseases.
7. Ensure environmental sustainability.
8. Develop a global partnership for development.

Through the Millennium Development Goals, the United Nations is addressing the many dimensions of poverty, thereby creating a context in which development can be achieved. All eight goals affect economic development, whether helping to alleviate poverty, create a healthy and educated labor force, protect limited resources, or develop a global *infrastructure* for industry and commerce.

Of all eight goals, the last is the one most closely associated with economic development. In order to create a global partnership for development, the United Nations has established seven specific objectives that, when met, should result in such a partnership. Those objectives are as follows:

- Develop further an open trading and financial system that is rule based, predictable, and nondiscriminatory. Includes a commitment to good governance, development and poverty reduction—nationally and internationally.

- Address the least developed countries' special needs. This includes tariff- and quota-free access for their exports; enhanced debt relief for heavily indebted poor countries; cancellation of official bilateral debt; and more generous official development assistance for countries committed to poverty reduction.

- Address the special needs of landlocked and small island developing nations.

The United Nations is seeking to reduce poverty around the world.

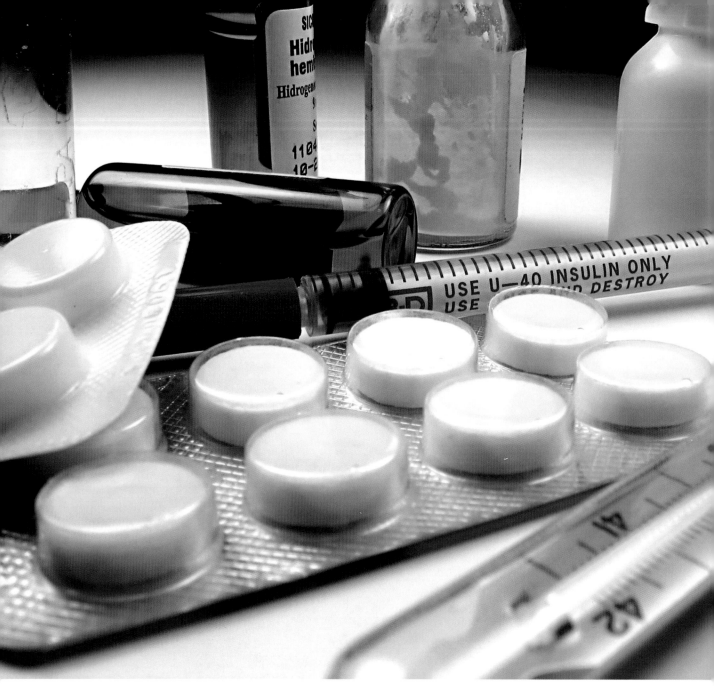

In the United States, we often take for granted that medicine and health care are easily available—but people in many parts of the world do not have access to the drugs they need for good health.

- Deal comprehensively with developing countries' debt problems through national and international measures to make debt sustainable in the long term.

- In cooperation with the developing countries, develop decent and productive work for youth.

- In cooperation with pharmaceutical companies, provide access to affordable essential drugs in developing countries.

- In cooperation with the private sector, make available the benefits of new technologies—especially information and communications technologies.

The United Nations has several official programs designed to assist countries in developing healthy economies. These programs have varying functions and responsibilities, but all share the common aim of achieving the Millennium Development Goals and their related objectives.

Official Programs

The primary UN body concerned with economic development is the United Nations Development Programme (UNDP). The UNDP is the UN's global development network, working to connect countries to knowledge, experience, and resources to help them create their own solutions to global and national development challenges. The UNDP is responsible for assisting developing countries to attract and apply aid effectively. In all areas, the UNDP encourages the protection of human rights and gender equality.

The UNDP helps countries integrate the Millennium Development Goals into their individual national development strategy. The UNDP can help development in these countries to be more effective by ensuring greater awareness of poverty, expanding access to productive assets and economic opportunities, and coordinating aid programs with countries' international economic and financial policies. The UNDP is also working to reform unfair trade practices, provide debt relief, and promote investment to give people of the world's poorest nations access to the global marketplace.

Another important UN program is the United Nations Industrial Development Organization (UNIDO). First organized in 1966, UNIDO is responsible for promoting industrialization

The United Nations works with people in third-world countries to promote the economy.

throughout the developing world. UNIDO helps to accomplish this goal by working with some of the world's poorest countries and countries with economies in transition to deliver critical skills, information, and technology to promote the growth of employment, a competitive economy, and a sound environment.

Promoting Development

For economic growth to take place, the health of the society as a whole must be strengthened. The United Nations can play an important role in the developing world by simply providing an environment in which development can take place. The UN's many specialized agencies are hard at work in the so-called ***third-world nations***, promoting peace and stability.

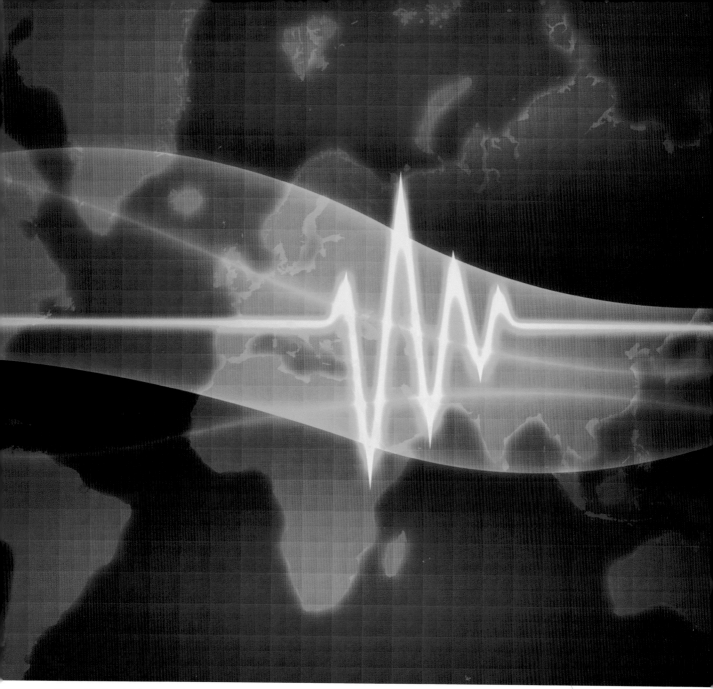

The United Nations keeps track of the world's financial pulse—and seeks to promote healthy economic growth.

The United Nations works with both the World Bank Group and regional banks to extend credit to poor nations.

The UN's primary function of promoting peace and security for the people of the world is essential to development, as armed conflict is devastating to most individuals' economic security. Working toward democracy is another key component in assisting development. By strengthening electoral and legislative systems, improving access to justice, and eliminating governmental corruption, the United Nations can help to provide a more favorable environment for investment and enterprise.

The United Nations also promotes development through its efforts in the area of crisis prevention and recovery. Serious crises such as the 2004 tsunami in Asia can have a devastating effect on emergent economies. By having resources in place to prevent manmade crises such as war or terrorist attack, and an effective response mechanism to unforeseen catastrophes such as famine, disease, or a natural disaster, the United Nations can protect the often-delicate stability of nations in the developing world.

Lending for Development and Stability

The development banks of today were originally conceived in the years of reconstruction that followed World War II. A group of these development banks—the International Bank for Reconstruction and Development (IBRD), the International Finance Corporation (IFC), the International Development Corporation, the Multilateral Investment Guarantee Agency, and the International Centre for Settlement of Investment Disputes—now make up the World Bank Group. The World Bank is the primary source of funding to poor nations seeking **capital** for development.

Loans are also available from a number of regional development banks, which were established to provide loans and development assistance on a more localized scale. These include the Inter-American Development Bank, the Asian Development Bank, the African Development Bank, and the European Investment Bank. The European Bank for Reconstruction and Development was added in 1991. There are also several subregional development banks, particularly in the Latin American and Caribbean region, as well as several Arab institutions.

The availability of credit to poor nations is critical for the achievement of the Millennium Development Goals. The flow of cash from the wealthier, industrialized nations of the world to the impoverished nations of the underdeveloped world is a cornerstone of UN economic policy. New enterprise cannot succeed without money, and this enterprise is essential if the world's poorest countries are to have a position in the global marketplace.

The United Nations invests in the global economy in order to build a more peaceful world.

While the UN-affiliated development banks provide loans on the national level, the United Nations also provides for lending on a smaller scale. The United Nations Capital Development Fund (UNCDF) lends small sums to individuals who wish to start or expand small businesses. This has proven to be an effective way to fight poverty and enhance stability. The UNCDF supports small banks in poor countries so they can lend capital to *entrepreneurs* who do not qualify for loans from commercial banks because they lack *collateral*.

Together, these UN efforts work together to build a healthier global economy—which in turn, leads to a more peaceful world. This is not all the United Nations does, however, when it comes to economic development.

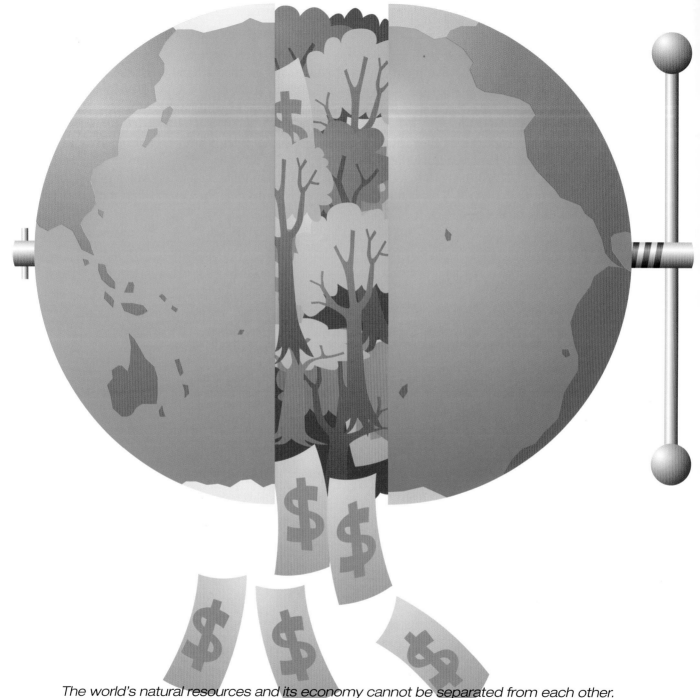

The world's natural resources and its economy cannot be separated from each other.

Chapter **2**

Sustainable Development

In 1987, the United Nations defined sustainable development as "development that meets the needs of the present without compromising the ability of future generations to meet their own needs." Basically, the concept states that people can't use up the Earth's limited potential today if they want human life to thrive in the future. Ultimately, no economy can thrive if the environment is unhealthy.

The UN and the Global Marketplace: Economic Developments

The origins of sustainable development as a philosophy can be found in the environmental movements of 1960s Europe and North America. As environmental concerns gained increasing attention throughout the decade, governments across the industrialized world began to feel pressure to address the ecological impact of commerce. In 1972, the United Nations held the Conference on the Human Environment in Stockholm, Sweden. This was the first of several international meetings focusing specifically on the environment and development. Each made important contributions to the movement for sustainable development.

The Stockholm Declaration

The Conference on the Human Environment was the first international diplomatic gathering to address human activities in relationship to the environment. The conference was responsible for the creation of the United Nations Environment Programme and the drafting of the Stockholm Declaration. The Stockholm Declaration is the foundation upon which all further sustainable development programs have been based.

The declaration opens with a series of seven proclamations, intended to identify the challenges facing the global community and the work to be done. These read as follows:

1. Man is both creature and molder of his environment, which gives him physical sustenance and affords him the opportunity for intellectual, moral, social and spiritual growth. In the long and tortuous evolution of the human race on this planet a stage has been reached when, through the rapid acceleration of science and technology, man has acquired the power to transform his environment in countless ways and on an unprecedented scale. Both aspects of man's environment, the natural and the man-made, are essential to his well-being and to the enjoyment of basic human rights, the right to life itself.

2. The protection and improvement of the human environment is a major issue which affects the well-being of peoples and economic development throughout the world; it is the urgent desire of the peoples of the whole world and the duty of all Governments.

3. Man has constantly to sum up experience and go on discovering, inventing, creating and advancing. In our time, man's capability to transform his surroundings, if used wisely, can bring to all peoples the benefits of development and the opportunity to

Stockholm was the site of the first international conference on the environment in 1972.

Mining has depleted many of the Earth's resources.

Industry is one of the biggest causes of dangerous levels of pollution in the air.

enhance the quality of life. Wrongly or heedlessly applied, the same power can do incalculable harm to human beings and the human environment. We see around us growing evidence of man-made harm in many regions of the earth: dangerous levels of pollution in water, air, earth and living beings; major and undesirable disturbances to the ecological balance of the **biosphere**; destruction and depletion of irreplaceable resources; and gross deficiencies, harmful to the physical, mental and social health of man, in the man-made environment, particularly in the living and working environment.

4. In the developing countries most of the environmental problems are caused by underdevelopment. Millions continue to live far below the minimum levels required for a decent human existence, deprived of adequate food and clothing, shelter and educa-

tion, health and sanitation. Therefore, the developing countries must direct their efforts to development, bearing in mind their priorities and the need to safeguard and improve the environment. For the same purpose, the industrialized countries should make efforts to reduce the gap between themselves and the developing countries. In the industrialized countries, environmental problems are generally related to industrialization and technological development.

5. The natural growth of population continuously presents problems for the preservation of the environment, and adequate policies and measures should be adopted, as appropriate, to face these problems. Of all things in the world, people are the most precious. It is the people that propel social progress, create social wealth, develop science and technology and, through their hard work, continuously transform the human environment. Along with social progress and the advance of production, science and technology, the capability of man to improve the environment increases with each passing day.

6. A point has been reached in history when we must shape our actions throughout the world with a more prudent care for their environmental consequences. Through ignorance or indifference we can do massive and irreversible harm to the earthly environment on which our life and well-being depend. Conversely, through fuller knowledge and wiser action, we can achieve for ourselves and our posterity a better life in an environment more in keeping with human needs and hopes. There are broad vistas for the enhancement of environmental quality and the creation of a good life. What is needed is an enthusiastic but calm state of mind and intense but orderly work. For the purpose of attaining freedom in the world of nature, man must use knowledge to build, in collaboration with nature, a better environment. To defend and improve the human environment for present and future generations has become an imperative goal for mankind—a goal to be pursued together with, and in harmony with, the established and fundamental goals of peace and of worldwide economic and social development.

7. To achieve this environmental goal will demand the acceptance of responsibility by citizens and communities and by enterprises and institutions at every level, all sharing equitably in common efforts. Individuals in all walks of life as well as organizations in many fields, by their values and the sum of their actions, will shape the world environment of the future.

Living in harmony with the environment is essential to human well-being.

The Stockholm Declaration affirms that human beings have a special responsibility to care for the Earth.

The declaration then lists twenty-six common principles, defining the obligations of nations and governments in regard to environmental concerns. These form the basis for all further conventions relating to sustainable development. These principles highlight the responsibilities of Member States across a broad spectrum of issues.

Principle 1

Man has the fundamental right to freedom, equality and adequate conditions of life, in an environment of a quality that permits a life of dignity and well-being, and he bears a solemn responsibility to protect and improve the environment for present and future generations.

In this respect, policies promoting or perpetuating apartheid, racial segregation, discrimination, colonial and other forms of oppression and foreign domination stand condemned and must be eliminated.

Principle 2

The natural resources of the earth, including the air, water, land, flora and fauna and especially representative samples of natural ecosystems, must be safeguarded for the benefit of present and future generations through careful planning or management, as appropriate.

Principle 3

The capacity of the earth to produce vital renewable resources must be maintained and, wherever practicable, restored or improved.

Principle 4

Man has a special responsibility to safeguard and wisely manage the heritage of wildlife and its habitat, which are now gravely imperiled by a combination of adverse factors. Nature conservation, including wildlife, must therefore receive importance in planning for economic development.

Principle 5

The nonrenewable resources of the earth must be employed in such a way as to guard against the danger of their future exhaustion and to ensure that benefits from such employment are shared by all mankind.

Principle 6

The discharge of toxic substances or of other substances and the release of heat, in such quantities or concentrations as to exceed the capacity of the environment to render them harmless, must be halted in order to ensure that serious or irreversible damage is not

Inadequately maintained oil tankers put the Earth's seas at risk.

inflicted upon ecosystems. The just struggle of the peoples of all countries against pollution should be supported.

Principle 7

States shall take all possible steps to prevent pollution of the seas by substances that are liable to create hazards to human health, to harm living resources and marine life, to damage amenities or to interfere with other legitimate uses of the sea.

Principle 8

Economic and social development is essential for ensuring a favorable living and working environment for man and for creating conditions on earth that are necessary for the improvement of the quality of life.

Principle 9

Environmental deficiencies generated by the conditions of under-development and natural disasters pose grave problems and can best be remedied by accelerated development through the transfer of substantial quantities of financial and technological assistance as a supplement to the domestic effort of the developing countries and such timely assistance as may be required.

Principle 10

For the developing countries, stability of prices and adequate earnings for primary commodities and raw materials are essential to environmental management, since economic factors as well as ecological processes must be taken into account.

Principle 11

The environmental policies of all States should enhance and not adversely affect the present or future development potential of developing countries, nor should they hamper the attainment of better living conditions for all, and appropriate steps should be taken by States and international organizations with a view to reaching agreement on meeting the possible national and international economic consequences resulting from the application of environmental measures.

Principle 12

Resources should be made available to preserve and improve the environment, taking into account the circumstances and particular requirements of developing countries and any costs which may emanate from their incorporating environmental safeguards into their development planning and the need for making available to them, upon their request, additional international technical and financial assistance for this purpose.

Principle 13

In order to achieve a more rational management of resources and thus to improve the environment, States should adopt an integrated and coordinated approach to their development planning so as to ensure that development is compatible with the need to protect and improve environment for the benefit of their population.

Principle 14

Rational planning constitutes an essential tool for reconciling any conflict between the needs of development and the need to protect and improve the environment.

Principle 15

Planning must be applied to human settlements and urbanization with a view to avoiding adverse effects on the environment and obtaining maximum social, economic and environmental benefits for all. In this respect projects which are designed for colonialist and racist domination must be abandoned.

Europe's windmills are examples of nations working together to care for the environment.

The United Nations works with farmers in Thailand to help them learn to increase the productivity of their fields without exhausting the soil's fertility.

Principle 16

Demographic policies which are without prejudice to basic human rights and which are deemed appropriate by Governments concerned should be applied in those regions where the rate of population growth or excessive population concentrations are likely to have adverse effects on the environment of the human environment and impede development.

Principle 17

Appropriate national institutions must be entrusted with the task of planning, managing or controlling the 9 environmental resources of States with a view to enhancing environmental quality.

Principle 18

Science and technology, as part of their contribution to economic and social development, must be applied to the identification, avoidance and control of environmental risks and the solution of environmental problems and for the common good of mankind.

Principle 19

Education in environmental matters, for the younger generation as well as adults, giving due consideration to the underprivileged, is essential in order to broaden the basis for an enlightened opinion and responsible conduct by individuals, enterprises and communities in protecting and improving the environment in its full human dimension. It is also essential that mass media of communications avoid contributing to the deterioration of the environment, but, on the contrary, disseminates information of an educational nature on the need to protect and improve the environment in order to enable man to develop in every respect.

Principle 20

Scientific research and development in the context of environmental problems, both national and multinational, must be promoted in all countries, especially the developing countries. In this connection, the free flow of up-to-date scientific information and transfer of experience must be supported and assisted, to facilitate the solution of environmental problems; environmental technologies should be made available to developing countries on terms which would encourage their wide dissemination without constituting an economic burden on the developing countries.

Principle 21

States have, in accordance with the Charter of the United Nations and the principles of international law, the sovereign right to exploit their own resources pursuant to their own environmental policies, and the responsibility to ensure that activities within their jurisdiction or control do not cause damage to the environment of other States or of areas beyond the limits of national jurisdiction.

Principle 22

States shall cooperate to develop further the international law regarding liability and compensation for the victims of pollution and other environmental damage caused by activities within the jurisdiction or control of such States to areas beyond their jurisdiction.

Principle 23

Without prejudice to such criteria as may be agreed upon by the international community, or to standards which will have to be determined nationally, it will be essential in all cases to consider the systems of values prevailing in each country, and the extent of the applicability of standards which are valid for the most advanced countries but which may be inappropriate and of unwarranted social cost for the developing countries.

Principle 24

International matters concerning the protection and improvement of the environment should be handled in a cooperative spirit by all countries, big and small, on an equal footing.

A sandstorm in Kenya demonstrates that environmental issues can create great hardship for a nation's people.

The world's nations met in Rio de Janeiro to establish an international partnership to protect the Earth's environment.

Cooperation through multilateral or bilateral arrangements or other appropriate means is essential to effectively control, prevent, reduce and eliminate adverse environmental effects resulting from activities conducted in all spheres, in such a way that due account is taken of the sovereignty and interests of all States.

Principle 25

States shall ensure that international organizations play a coordinated, efficient and dynamic role for the protection and improvement of the environment.

Principle 26

Man and his environment must be spared the effects of nuclear weapons and all other means of mass destruction. States must strive to reach prompt agreement, in the relevant international organs, on the elimination and complete destruction of such weapons.

In the decades that followed the Stockholm Declaration, other steps were taken to address environmental concerns within the context of economic development. In 1986, the United Nations appointed a World Commission on Environment and Development to research important areas of environmental damage around the globe. Led by Norway's prime minister, Gro Harlem Brundtland, the commission conducted its research and reported its findings along with some proposed solutions. Officially titled *Our Common Future: Report of the World Commission on Environment and Development*, the Brundtland report brought the idea of sustainable development to the attention of the global community once more and called for international cooperation to combat growing environmental problems.

The Rio Earth Summit

The United Nations held the 1992 Rio Summit in hopes of building upon the foundation laid in the Stockholm Declaration. Public awareness and debate around environmental issues peaked with a number of new agreements dealing with a wide variety of issues, including **biodiversity** and climate change.

A series of twenty-seven principles were proclaimed at Rio with the goal of establishing a new international partnership through the creation of new levels of cooperation among nations, to

Sustainable development encourages third-world countries to grow economically without depleting their resources (including farmland) in the process.

produce international agreements that respect the interests of all people and protect the best interests of the world's environmental and developmental system. The Rio Declaration created a framework of action for sustainable development in the twenty-first century that eventually became known as Agenda 21. The United Nations also formed the Commission on Sustainable Development (CSD) to monitor implementation of agreements reached in Rio.

In May 2000, environmental ministers from all over the world met in Malmo, Sweden, to review important and emerging environmental issues and to plan for the future. This led in August 2002 to the World Summit on Sustainable Development (WSSD), held in Johannesburg, South Africa. This conference, also known as "Rio + 10," focused on new scientific evidence of global environmental change. In the Summit's Political Declaration, world leaders promised to commit themselves to working together, united by a common determination to save our planet, promote human development, and achieve universal prosperity and peace. Leaders also pledged to speed up efforts to accomplish the time-bound, socioeconomic, and environmental targets contained in the implementation plan.

Although the United Nations has made considerable progress in promoting sustainable development worldwide, much debate remains—not only among nations, but among varying interest groups, industries, and nongovernmental organizations (NGOs)—as to the best way to realize these goals. While the Johannesburg Declaration made a strong stand for sustainable development, some key areas were not addressed due to a lack of clear *consensus*. Most notably, summit negotiations were stalled in three prominent areas: agriculture subsidies, energy interests, and exemptions from some environmental protections for the poorest countries.

Despite these issues, Agenda 21 is an ongoing UN plan that builds the global economy by protecting the environment.

Agenda 21 is the UN model for economic development in the twenty-first century.

Chapter **3**

Agenda 21

Agenda 21 is the UN blueprint for sustainable development. A comprehensive plan to achieve sustainable development globally, nationally, and locally, Agenda 21 describes the responsibilities of the United Nations, individual governments, and major groups in every area in which humans impact the environment. Agenda 21 was named because of its significance as a model for economic growth in the twenty-first century.

The UN and the Global Marketplace: Economic Developments

Development of Agenda 21

The full text of Agenda 21 was drafted through a painstaking process of negotiation that began in 1989. Revealed at the 1992 United Nations Conference on Environment and Development (the Rio Earth Summit), 179 governments voted to adopt the program. Outlined in the Rio Declaration, Agenda 21 is comprised of twenty-seven principles designed to address every area of economic development.

Agenda 21's forty chapters are divided into four sections. The first addresses social and economic issues such as combating poverty, changing consumption habits, population and *demographic* dynamics, promoting health, promoting sustainable settlement patterns, and integrating environment and development into decision-making. The second section is concerned with conservation and management of resources for development, including atmospheric protection, combating *deforestation*, protecting fragile environments, conservation of biodiversity, and control of pollution. Section three seeks to strengthen the roles of children and youth, women, NGOs, local authorities, businesses, and workers. Section four describes the specific means by which the plan should be put into practice.

In December 1992, the UN General Assembly established the Commission on Sustainable Development (CSD) to oversee the implementation of Agenda 21 and report on the progress being made on the global, national, and local level in meeting its objectives. The commission is composed of fifty-three members elected to three-year terms and meets once a year for a period of two to three weeks. It reports to the Economic and Social Council and, through it, to the Second Committee of the General Assembly.

The Economic and Social Council elects CSD members from among UN Member States. Thirteen members are elected from Africa, eleven from Asia, ten from Latin America and the Caribbean, six from Eastern Europe, and thirteen from Western Europe and other nations. One-third of the members are elected annually, and outgoing members are eligible for reelection. Other countries, UN organizations, and accredited intergovernmental organizations and NGOs are welcome to attend CSD sessions as observers.

The CSD has several important functions. Originally, it was designed to have a rather limited role in evaluating progress toward the implementation of Agenda 21. However, in recent years it has been assigned greater importance in developing policy and working as a liaison between governments, the international community, and the major groups identified in Agenda 21 as key actors outside the central government with a significant role to play in the move toward sustainable development. These groups include women, youth, *indigenous* peoples, NGOs, workers and trade unions, business and industry, scientists, and farmers.

Agenda 21's second section is concerned with protecting the world's forests. Lumbering has devastated the forests of Tasmania in Australia.

U.S. president George W. Bush did not attend Earth Summit in 2002.

In 1997, the UN General Assembly held a special session to review five years of progress toward the implementation of Agenda 21. In this session, known as Rio+5, the Assembly acknowledged that progress was "uneven" and identified troubling new issues including increasing *globalization*, widening inequalities in income, and a continued deterioration of the global environment. A new General Assembly resolution was drafted promising further action.

A UN-organized World Summit on Sustainable Development (also called the Earth Summit) took place in Johannesburg, South Africa, from August 26 to September 4, 2002, to further discuss sustainable development issues. Held ten years after the World Summit in Rio de Janeiro, the Earth Summit gathered a number of leaders of nations, businesses, and NGOs. Once again, a resolution was drafted promising further action in implementing Agenda 21. Critics, however, draw attention to the inability of the United Nations to enforce the provisions of Agenda 21. They also cite a lack of commitment from the world's wealthiest nations. U.S. president George W. Bush did not attend the Johannesburg Summit; those in attendance booed U.S. secretary of state Colin Powell.

Agenda 21 in Action

Agenda 21 was intended to outline appropriate action at the international, national, regional, and local levels. Many governments have legislated or advised that local authorities take steps to implement the plan locally, as recommended in chapter 28 of the document. The resulting programs are known as "Local Agenda 21." Agenda 21 also provides for action by NGOs. This provides a framework for action when there is little or no political will to make sustainable development a priority. The tiny nation of Slovenia in Central Europe, provides an excellent example of how Agenda 21 was meant to function.

In 1990, Slovenia became a nation in transition as it shifted from a communist country to an independent state with a *free-market economy*. Although the current changes in social and economic systems present a unique opportunity for the implementation of sustainable development, the Slovene government has been slow to enforce existing environmental legislation or to work more aggressively toward sustainable development out of fear that it could slow economic growth.

Agenda 21 for Slovenia was born in response to fears that the Slovenian government was not aware of the importance of environmental issues and of the commitments made in Rio. Coordinated by Umanotera, the Slovenian Foundation for Sustainable Development, the project was initiated in 1995 with a brief survey of Slovenian NGOs to determine how familiar they were with key international principles of sustainable development.

Slovenia's capital city; the United Nations uses the principles of Agenda 21 to help this small new nation grow.

The first national-level workshop, held later that year, welcomed twenty-four members from nineteen Slovenian NGOs and a number of observers from the Slovene government. Workshop participants identified key environmental problems and obstacles to sustainability in Slovenia. These problems occurred within three dimensions of activity: cultural, political, and economic. It was determined that "solutions" to specific problems in one area simply emerged as new problems somewhere else—or in the future. So to harmonize necessary changes with principles of sustainable development, reform would be approached on all three levels simultaneously, with full awareness of the laws applying to interrelationships within the system.

Several additional workshops were held dealing with problems on the local level before a second national workshop was convened. The second national workshop produced a strategy for sustainable development titled "Agenda 21 for Slovenia: A Contribution of Non-Governmental Organizations." The document was based on the discussions held in the workshops, with an in-depth analysis of the present state of development in various sectors of Slovenia.

Although this process was neither initiated nor sponsored by the government, the resulting development blueprint has prompted governmental action. Pavel Gantar, Slovene minister of

Because the Earth's resources are limited, sustainable development is a vital concept.

A field of hops, used in the production of beer, grows in Slovenia.

environment, announced that the ministry would use the document in drafting a national environmental protection program. Zare Pregelj, chairman of the Parliamentary Council on Environment and Infrastructure, proposed that parliament study the plan and commission a more in-depth study on transition toward sustainable development.

Agenda 21 for Slovenia has already seen some modest successes. For example, NGOs in Maribor are working to ease traffic and reduce pollution by making the city bicycle-friendly, modeling it on a project in the nearby Austrian city of Graz. Nature conservation programs are also showing positive results. Skocjanski Zatok on the Adriatic Coast is Slovenia's only wetland and is now being turned into a protected area.

One of the recommendations from the Agenda 21 for Slovenia workshops was to develop a series of small *pilot projects*. Such projects demonstrating principles of sustainable development in practice offer an opportunity to build momentum and overcome resistance to change. As a result, a three-year project was designed to "adopt" an existing corporate farm and aid it in its conversion to *organic* farming and *ecotourism*. Not only can it serve as a demonstration farm, but it can also offer valuable knowledge and experience gained in the process of transition.

The spirit of Agenda 21 as a means to provide a healthy and prosperous future for generations to come can be summed up in this statement by Agenda 21 for Slovenia:

Respecting the natural and cultural properties of our land, we can reach a considerably higher degree of development and quality of life. A combination of traditional approaches and modern technology will assist us in living within the limits of environmental space for Slovenia and the planet Earth. . . . With this document, we hope to present an optimistic concept of a human society as a self-regulating system, capable of balancing itself with nature while not having to sacrifice economic development or quality of life. Outdated social and economic structures will be the only necessary "sacrifices" in this process.

Human beings' lives are enriched when nations' economies are developed.

Chapter **4**

Development Programs

The UNDP is the United Nation's primary body providing economic development. Established in 1965, the UNDP was created to unify the operations of the Expanded Program of Technical Assistance and the United Nations Special Fund, which continued as separate components of UNDP until full unification in 1971. The UNDP is the chief source of technical assistance to developing countries, with most of its aid coming in the form of consultants' services, equipment, and fellowships for advanced study abroad.

The UN and the Global Marketplace: Economic Developments

Thousands of projects in areas as diverse as resource planning, training institutes, the application of modern technology to development, and the building of the economic and social infrastructure are supported by the UNDP. It also dispenses UN special purpose funds for resource exploration, combating ***desertification***, and technology development, as well as working with UN-associated agencies involved in development activities.

The UNDP is funded by voluntary contributions from UN members. The agency not only provides its own assistance but assists developing countries to attract and use aid effectively. Its various programs focus on work in five areas of critical importance:

- democratic governance
- poverty reduction
- crisis prevention and recovery
- energy and environment
- HIV/AIDS

The UNDP is also responsible for generating the Human Development Report (HDR). The HDR was first launched in 1990 with the objective of putting individuals back at the center of the development process in terms of economic debate, policy, and ***advocacy***. The idea was to go beyond income when evaluating the level of people's long-term well-being.

Evaluating Human Development

The HDR is an independent report commissioned by the UNDP. However, it is the work of a selected team of leading scholars, development practitioners, and members of the Human Development Report Office. The report is translated into more than a dozen languages and issued in more than a hundred countries annually.

Each year the report focuses on a specific topic or theme in the current development debate, providing important analysis and policy recommendations. People around the world have implemented the report's proposals. The value of the HDR and its approach is shown by the publication of national human development reports at the national level in more than 120 countries.

The HDR has developed four separate indexes to evaluate human development. These statistical rankings—the Human Development Index (HDI), the Gender-Related Development Index, the Gender Empowerment Measure, and the Human Poverty Index—are often important in determining a country's need for foreign aid. The HDI is a comparative measure of poverty, literacy, education, life expectancy, and other factors for countries worldwide. It is a standard means

The HDR evaluates the development and needs of various groups of human beings, including these villagers from the Ovahimbo Tribe in Africa.

The HDI evaluates child welfare in the world's nations.

The HDR gives the United Nations a tool for measuring the well-being of groups of people around the globe.

of measuring well-being, especially child welfare. The United States ranked tenth on the HDI for 2005.

The compilation of these statistics and reports by the UNDP is critical to evaluating development and progress around the globe. The data collected assists in creating development agendas and priorities that direct international attention toward the economic, social, political, and cultural issues that oppress people in the world's developing nations. The HDR is an important tool for policy analysis that works by identifying inequities and measuring growth.

Democratic Governance

Democracy is good for the economy—and democratic governance is essential for the achievement of the Millennium Development Goals. It provides "an enabling environment" for the realization of the goals and, in particular, the elimination of poverty. The critical importance of democratic governance in the developing world was highlighted at the Millennium Summit of 2000, where the world's leaders pledged to "spare no effort to promote democracy and strengthen the rule of law, as well as respect for all internationally recognized human rights and fundamental freedoms, including the right to development." By improving the quality of democratic institutions and processes, the United Nations hopes to reduce poverty, better protect the environment, and promote human development.

The UNDP works to develop institutions and processes that are more responsive to the needs of ordinary citizens, especially the poor. The UNDP brings people together—within nations and internationally—to promote participation in government and improve accountability and effectiveness at all levels. Countries receive assistance to strengthen their *electoral* and legislative systems, improve access to justice and public administration, and develop an enhanced ability to deliver basic services to those most in need.

The UNDP provides support and assistance to countries that require aid in instituting electoral processes. By supporting sustainable development, as well as electoral processes and institutions that allow all citizens to elect their representatives freely and hold them accountable for commitments, a more favorable environment is created to attract foreign aid and investment.

In societies undergoing rapid change as an effect of globalization or political transition, well-organized administrative services can simplify the implementation of national development plans. The UNDP helps to build public service structures that are cost-efficient and results-oriented, and that answer to the citizens they are intended to serve. Honest management of public financial resources constitutes one of the most fundamental responsibilities of government. Preventing and combating corruption is a major challenge for many governments in the world, particularly those in developing countries and for economies in transition. Minimizing corruption is critical to stimulating investment, reducing poverty, and promoting sustainable development.

Poverty Reduction

In accordance with the Millennium Development Goals, developing countries are working to create their own national poverty-reduction strategies based on local needs and priorities. The UNDP speaks for these poor nations and helps to make their efforts more effective through providing a greater voice for poor people, creating greater access to productive assets and economic opportunities, and coordinating national poverty programs with international economic policies.

The UNDP sponsors pilot projects, connects developing countries to the world's best practices and resources, promotes the importance of women in development, and brings governments, civil society, and outside investors together to better coordinate their efforts. Such actions to

Mozambicans wait to vote in a UN-assisted election in 1994; democracy is good for the economy!

The December 2004 tsunami brought a tidal wave of new poverty to Banda Aceh in Indonesia.

reform trade, grant debt relief, and promote investment all help support national poverty reduction and make globalization work better for poor people. Besides its advocacy work, the UNDP focuses on policy advisory services that seek to ensure that both national and global trade, debt, and capital flow policies function on the basis of human development concerns.

Crisis Prevention and Recovery

Poor countries are unusually vulnerable to violent conflicts and can be more severely affected by their aftermath. Natural disasters—like the December 2004 tsunami that devastated Asia—can erase decades of development and further ingrain poverty and inequality. With a network of global partners, the UNDP develops and shares innovative approaches to conflict prevention and peace-building, disaster relief, and post-crisis recovery. The UNDP is on hand in most of the developing world to organize crisis prevention and recovery efforts and to help bridge the gap between emergency relief and long-term development.

Its support for democratic governance and poverty reduction has given the UNDP a well-established track record. From Mozambique and Afghanistan to Guatemala and Albania, the UNDP has played a major role in helping countries develop a viable agenda for economic development by promoting the rule of law and fair governance, working toward justice and security, *demobilizing* soldiers, reducing the flow of small arms, eliminating environmental hazards such as land mines, and putting war-affected people back to work.

The UNDP has worked from Goma, in the Democratic Republic of Congo, to Gujarat, India, to provide quick and effective response to natural disasters. When short-term humanitarian aid is phasing out, the UNDP provides sustainable recovery initiatives by directing attention to disaster relief and preparations for the rebuilding process. Such crisis response is at the core of the UNDP mandate for poverty elimination and democratic governance.

Energy and Environment

Effective energy and environmental policy are essential for economic development. The world's poor are disproportionately affected by environmental damage and lack of access to clean, affordable energy. Issues such as climate change, loss of biodiversity, and ozone layer depletion are international in scope and cannot be addressed by countries acting alone. The UNDP assists countries to strengthen their ability to address these challenges at the global, national, and community levels.

AIDS is a worldwide problem—but it is a crisis in Africa.

The UNDP's Energy and Environment Practice works in six priority areas:

- frameworks and strategies for sustainable development
- effective water governance
- access to sustainable energy services
- sustainable land management to combat desertification and land degradation
- conservation and sustainable use of biodiversity
- national/sectoral policy and planning to control emissions of ozone depleting substances and persistent organic pollutants

HIV/AIDS

HIV/AIDS affects economic development worldwide. Striking many during their most productive working years, HIV/AIDS is uniquely devastating, as it increases poverty and reverses any development successes. In order to support countries most tragically affected by the HIV/AIDS epidemic, the UNDP promotes responses that incorporate HIV/AIDS prevention in national, state, and local development plans. In partnership with the World Bank, the UNDP provides technical support to assist countries to more effectively integrate the fight against HIV/AIDS into their poverty reduction schemes. In addition, the UNDP helps countries generate trade, health, and intellectual property legislation for dependable access to low-cost, quality AIDS medicines.

Economic development is a complicated goal, involving many issues, including the environment, health, and effective response to wars and disasters. These issues cannot be addressed without financial support; it takes money to produce money.

An immense chasm lies between the lives of people in poor nations and the lives of those who live in rich countries.

5

Financing Development

As the United Nations seeks to implement its ambitious Millennium Development Goals, a primary concern is how such development can be financed. The gap between the poorest and the richest nations of the world has continued to widen. Various aspects of international policy require reform in order for developing countries to benefit from the process of globalization.

ODA provides money for world development.

Recent changes have been made to address the ever-growing need for development dollars. The first steps toward reform came from the International Conference on Financing for Development, which was held in March 2002 in Monterrey, Mexico.

Known simply as the Monterrey Conference, this first UN-hosted conference to address key financial and development issues attracted fifty heads of state or government, over two hundred high-level ministers, leaders from the ***private sector***, and senior officials of all the major intergovernmental financial, trade, and economic organizations. The far-reaching plan of action drafted at this conference is known as the Monterrey Consensus, in which countries with developed, developing, and transition economies pledged to undertake important actions in domestic, international, and systemic policy matters.

Official Development Assistance

Official Development Assistance (ODA) is still the largest source of aid to underdeveloped countries. ODA has its roots in the aftermath of World War II. In 1944, the forty-four Allied nations gathered to form the United Nations Monetary and Financial Conference in Bretton Woods, New Hampshire. This conference led to the establishment of the International Bank for Reconstruction and Development (World Bank) and the International Monetary Fund (IMF). These still constitute some of the largest sources of ODA.

ODA is money to be used for development. Although most often the aid will be in the form of a loan, the loan is made more on the basis of need than credit worthiness. The loan part of the aid received will have low interest terms and a long repayment period. To qualify as ODA, at least a quarter of the money received will never have to be paid back.

Governments give this money through individual countries' international aid agencies, through institutions such as the World Bank, and through individuals involved with NGOs such

Definition of ODA

"Flows to developing countries and multilateral institutions provided by official agencies, including state and local governments, or by their executive agencies, each transaction of which meets the following test: a) it is administered with the promotion of the economic development and welfare of developing countries as its main objective, and b) it is concessional in character and contains a grant element of at least 25 percent."

The UN and the Global Marketplace: Economic Developments

According to the IMF's articles of agreement, "The purposes of the International Monetary Fund are:

i. To promote international monetary cooperation through a permanent institution which provides the machinery for consultation and collaboration on international monetary problems.

ii. To facilitate the expansion and balanced growth of international trade, and to contribute thereby to the promotion and maintenance of high levels of employment and real income and to the development of the productive resources of all members as primary objectives of economic policy.

iii. To promote exchange stability, to maintain orderly exchange arrangements among members, and to avoid competitive exchange depreciation.

iv. To assist in the establishment of a multilateral system of payments in respect of current transactions between members and in the elimination of foreign exchange restrictions which hamper the growth of world trade.

v. To give confidence to members by making the general resources of the Fund temporarily available to them under adequate safeguards, thus providing them with opportunity to correct maladjustments in their balance of payments without resorting to measures destructive of national or international prosperity.

vi. In accordance with the above, to shorten the duration and lessen the degree of disequilibrium in the international balances of payments of members.

The Fund shall be guided in all its policies and decisions by the purposes set forth in this Article."

as Care International or Oxfam. The wealthiest UN Member States have pledged to make specific amounts available as ODA in order to meet the Millennium Development Goals.

Following the Monterrey Conference, the United Nations established the Financing for Development Office. The mission of the Financing for Development Office is:

to provide effective secretariat support for sustained follow-up within the United Nations system to the agreements and commitments reached at the International Conference on Financing for Development, as contained in the Monterrey Consensus, as well as financing for development-related aspects of the outcomes of major United Nations conferences and summits in the economic and social fields, including the development goals set out in the United Nations Millennium Declaration.

The UN cannot meet its millennium goals without money from its richest members.

Experts from official and academic sectors meet to examine ways to reduce the world's poverty.

Within the United Nations, the major institutional players are the IMF, the World Bank, the World Trade Organization (WTO), and the UNDP. These institutions regularly meet to discuss the implementation of the Monterrey Consensus and projects on financing for development. In addition, the Financing for Development Office brings together experts from the official and private sectors, as well as academia and civil society, to examine issues related to the mobilization of resources for financing development and poverty reduction.

The economies of all the world's nations—and all their people as well—are linked together.

The UN and the Global Marketplace: Economic Developments

Multilateral Institutions

The World Bank, IMF, and WTO are ***multilateral*** institutions that provide development assistance. Developed in response to the need to rebuild after the devastation of World War II, these institutions now provide assistance to impoverished, war-torn, and disaster-stricken nations all over the world.

The World Bank is a crucial source of financial and technical assistance to developing countries. It is not a bank in the regular sense, since it is made up of two separate development institutions—the International Bank for Reconstruction and Development (IBRD) and the International Development Association (IDA)—owned by 184 UN member countries. Each of the World Bank's institution plays a different but vital role in the effort to do away with poverty and improve living standards worldwide. The IBRD focuses on loans to middle income and creditworthy poor countries, while the IDA focuses on grants to the poorest countries in the world. Together the two institutions provide low-interest loans, interest-free credit, and grants to developing countries for education, health, infrastructure, communications, and many other important purposes.

The IMF is the central institution of the international monetary system, the system of international payments and ***exchange rates*** among national currencies that enables business to take place internationally. It aims to prevent crises in the system by encouraging countries to adopt sound economic policies; it is also an actual fund that can be accessed by members needing temporary financing to address economic problems. Headquartered in Washington, D.C., it is governed by its membership of 184 countries.

The WTO deals with the rules of trade between nations at a global or near-global level. Made up of members from 184 different countries, its primary purpose is to help trade flow as freely as possible without creating undesirable side effects. In part, that means removing barriers to free trade. It also means ensuring that individuals, companies, and governments know what the trade rules are around the world, and to provide the world with stable and predictable trade practices.

The WTO is an important negotiating forum in which representatives from member nations try to resolve the trade problems they face with each other. Everything the WTO does is the result of negotiations. The majority of the WTO's current work comes from the 1986—1994 negotiations called the Uruguay Round and earlier negotiations under the General Agreement on Tariffs and Trade (GATT). Once a set of negotiations ends and the nations reach an agreement, each individual government must ***ratify*** the new laws. Such trade negotiations try to respect the nation's other treaty obligations, including UN resolutions.

Almost two-thirds of the WTO's members are developing countries. Their membership has become increasingly important as their numbers grow; first, because they are becoming more

The IMF regulates exchange rates for each nation's currency.

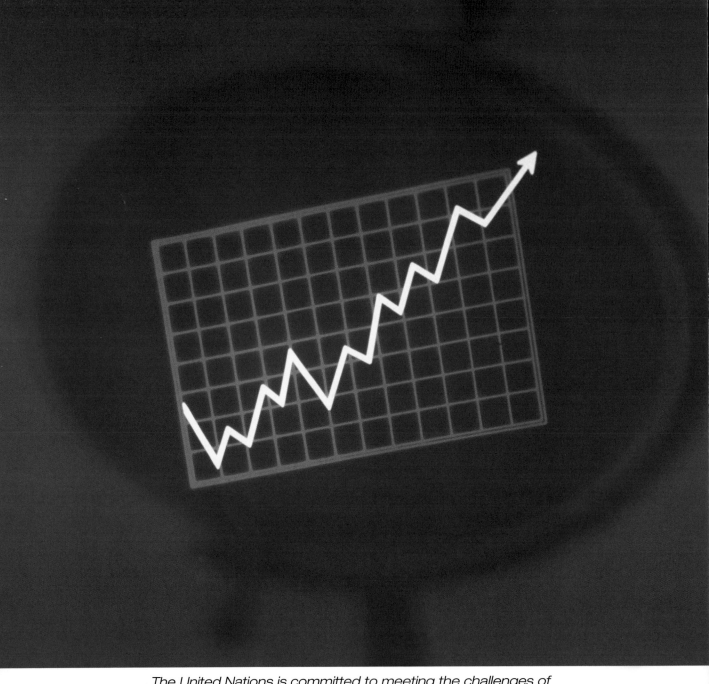

The United Nations is committed to meeting the challenges of development around the globe.

important in the global economy, and second, because trade is often the vital tool in their development efforts. The world's developing countries are a highly diverse group with very different views and concerns, so it is not always easy to reach an agreement.

The WTO assists developing countries in three ways:

1. Many WTO agreements include numerous provisions giving developing and least-developed countries special rights or extra *leniency*.
2. The WTO Secretariat has special legal advisers for assisting developing countries in any WTO dispute and for giving them legal counsel.
3. The WTO provides extensive education and technical assistance to countries with developing markets, helping them draft laws and implement policies favorable to trade.

The United Nations works very closely with the WTO to help developing countries. In October 1997, six international organizations including the IMF, the International Trade Centre, the United Nations Conference for Trade and Development, the UNDP, the World Bank, and the WTO launched the Integrated Framework, a joint technical assistance program exclusively for the world's least-developed countries.

Although aid is available in many forms and from many sources, the situation in much of the developing world remains grim. Far from the wealth and luxury of the Western world, people struggle daily with issues such as poverty, hunger, illiteracy, and disease. As the world's only truly global body, the United Nations has a special obligation to bring the needs of the world's most vulnerable to the attention of those with the means to help. Through its extensive network of official agencies, its power to affect its own extensive membership, and through cooperation with international institutions and aid agencies, the United Nations is committed to meeting the challenges of development around the globe.

Time Line

1944	The United Nations Monetary and Financial Conference is held in Bretton Woods, New Hampshire.
1945	The United Nations officially comes into existence.
1945	The World Bank institutions and the IMF are officially incorporated.
1965	The UNDP is established.
1972	The United Nations issues the Stockholm Declaration.
1990	The United Nations issues the first Human Development Report.
1990	The Human Development Index (HDI) is developed by Pakistani economist Mahbub ul Haq.
1992	The United Nations holds the Rio Earth Summit; it unveils Agenda 21.
1992	The Commission on Sustainable Development is established.
1993	The Human Development Report begins to use the HDI to rank countries.
1997	The General Assembly holds special "Rio+5" session to review progress toward implementing Agenda 21.
2000	The Millennium Summit takes place, and Millennium Development Goals are established.
2002	The World Summit on Sustainable Development is held in Johannesburg, South Africa.
2002	The International Conference on Financing for Development is held in Monterrey, Mexico.
November 2005	The Beijing Declaration on Renewable Energy for Sustainable Development is issued.
2006	The UN continues to work to build the economies of the world's nations.

Glossary

advocacy: Active support for a cause or position.

biodiversity: The range of organisms present in a given ecological community or system.

biosphere: The part of the world in which life can exist.

capital: Material wealth in the form of money or property.

collateral: Property or goods used as security against a loan and forfeited if the loan is not repaid.

consensus: General or widespread agreement among all members of a group.

deforestation: The practice of removing trees from an area of land.

demobilizing: Discharging personnel from the armed forces and sending them home.

demographic: Relating to the characteristics of a human population.

desertification: A process by which land becomes increasingly dry.

ecotourism: A form of tourism that strives to minimize ecological or other damage to areas visited for their natural or cultural interest.

electoral: Relating to elections.

entrepreneurs: People who set up and finance new commercial businesses to make a profit.

exchange rates: The rates that currency of one country can be exchanged for a unit of the currency of another country.

free-market economy: An economic system in which businesses operate without government control in matters such as pricing and wage levels.

globalization: The process by which social institutions become adopted on a worldwide scale.

indigenous: Native born to a region.

infrastructure: The large-scale public systems, services, and facilities of a country or region that are necessary for economic activity.

leniency: Punishment, judgment, or action that is not too severe.

multilateral: Many sided.

organic: Relating to agricultural practices that avoid the use of synthetic chemicals.

pilot projects: Projects used to test a process or product and to solve problems before the product or process is put to general use.

private sector: Ordinary people who are not formally involved with government.

ratify: To officially approve.

third-world nations: Countries outside the capitalist industrial nations of the first world and the industrialized nations of the communist second world.

Further Reading

Anderson, Sarah, ed. *Views from the South: The Effects of Globalization and the WTO on Third World Countries.* Oakland, Calif.: Food First, 2000.

Beckerman, Wilfred. *A Poverty of Reason: Sustainable Development and Economic Growth.* Oakland, Calif.: The Independent Institute, 2002.

Hawken, Paul. *Ecology of Commerce: A Declaration of Sustainability.* New York: HarperCollins, 1994.

Sachs, Jeffrey. *The End of Poverty: Economic Possibilities for Our Time.* New York: Penguin Group, 2005.

Sen, Amartya. *Development as Freedom.* New York: Knopf Publishing Group, 2000.

For More Information

Charter of the United Nations
www.un.org/aboutun/charter/index.html

International Monetary Fund
700 19th Street, N.W.
Washington, D.C. 20431
Tel.: (202) 623-7300
Fax: (202) 623-6278
http://www.imf.org/external

The United Nations
www.un.org

United Nations Cyberschoolbus
www.un.org/Pubs/CyberSchoolBus/index.asp

United Nations
Office of the Spokesman for the Secretary-General
United Nations, S-378
New York, NY 10017
Tel.: (212) 963-4475
Fax: (212) 963-7055

The World Bank
1818 H Street, N.W.
Washington, DC 20433 USA
Tel.: (202) 473-1000
Fax: (202) 477-6391
www.worldbank.org

World Trade Organization
Centre William Rappard
Rue de Lausanne 154

CH-1211 Geneva 21
Switzerland
Tel.: (41-22) 739 51 11
Fax: (41-22) 731 42 06
www.wto.org

Publisher's note:
The Web sites listed on these pages were active at the time of publication. The publisher is not responsible for Web sites that have changed their addresses or discontinued operation since the date of publication. The publisher will review and update the Web-site list upon each reprint.

Reports and Projects

Maps

• Using a map of the world, rank all the countries on the map according to the Human Development Index.

Reports

• Write a brief report on the formation of the World Bank or the IMF.
• Write a report on sustainable development.
• Write a brief report on the UNDP and its programs.

Biographies

Write a one-page biography on one of the following:

• Kofi Annan
• Mahbub ul Haq

Journal

• Choose a country that is ranked as one of the world's poorest nations according to the Human Development Index. Create a journal entry describing what your day might be like if you lived there. Would it make a big difference whether you were a boy or a girl? Why or why not?
• Study one of the development assistance programs that actually put UN workers on the ground. Write a journal entry describing your experience as an employee of the WHO doing work with HIV/AIDS-infected people or providing technical assistance in a country recently at war. How do you feel about your job?

Research Projects

• Learn about Local Agenda 21 and see if there are any projects going on near you.
• Find a nongovernmental organization that provides development assistance, such as Oxfam. Plan a service project that lets you and your friends assist them in their efforts.
• Research a recent event such as the tsunami in Asia or the war in Afghanistan and see what kind of development assistance the UN is providing.

• Imagine you are a representative from a developing country at the Rio Earth Summit. What proposals did you support? What parts of the Rio Declaration might you not agree with?

• Research the fall of communism in Eastern Europe. What kind of assistance did the UN provide those countries as they made the transition to a democratic form of government? Write a report about it.

Bibliography

Development Gateway. http://www.developmentgateway.org.

Eleventh Session of the UN Conference on Trade and Development. http://www.unctadxi.org, 2005.

Global Policy Forum. http://www.globalpolicy.org.

International Monetary Fund. http://www.imf.org.

Local Implementation of Agenda 21. http://www.cityshelter.org/13_mobil/04tend.htm.

Making Development Work.
   http://www.econ.nyu.edu/cvstarr/conferences/ForeignAid/papers/Banerjee.pdf.

Overseas Development Institute. http://www.odi.org.uk.

UN Non-governmental Liaison Service. http://www.un-ngls.org.

UNDP Human Development Report. http://hdr.undp.org, 2005.

United Nations. www.un.org.

United Nations Development Program. http://www.undp.org.

World Bank. http://www.worldbank.org.

World Trade Organization. http://www.wto.org.

Index

apartheid 29

biodiversity 39, 44, 63
Bush, George W. 47

Care International 68
climate 39
conservation 44, 51
corruption 58
crisis 17, 54, 61

debt relief 10, 13, 61
discrimination 29
disease 10, 75

economic development 10, 13, 19, 22, 26, 29,
    31, 35, 39, 43, 53
energy 41, 54, 61, 63
environmental sustainability 10, 22, 25, 31–32,
    43

famine 17
foreign domination 29

gender equality 10, 13, 54
global economy 19, 75

HIV/AIDS 10, 54, 63
human rights 13, 35
hunger 10

industrialization 26

malaria 10
maternal health 10

natural disasters 17, 31, 61
natural resources 29
nongovernmental organizations (NGOs) 41, 44,
    47, 48, 67
nuclear weapons 39

oppression 29
Oxfam 68

pollution 31, 63
poverty 10, 19, 44, 54, 57–58, 61, 71, 75
primary education 10

racial segregation 29

sanitation 26
social development 26, 31, 35
sustainable development 21–22, 25–26, 28–29,
    31–32, 35–36, 39, 41, 43, 44, 48–49, 51, 58,
    63

technological development 26, 31, 36, 51, 54
third-world nations 17
tsunami 17

United Nations
    Agenda 21 43–44, 47–49, 51
    Capital Development Fund (UNCDF) 19
    Charter 36
    Commission on Sustainable Development
        (CSD) 41, 44
    Conference on the Human Environment
        (Stockholm Declaration) 22, 25–26,
        27–29, 31–32, 35–36, 39, 41

United Nations (*Cont.*)

Development Program (UNDP) 13, 53–54, 57–58, 61, 63, 71

Economic and Social Council 44

General Assembly 44, 45

Financing for Development Office 68

Human Development Index (HDI) 54, 57

Human Development Report (HDR) 54

Industrial Development Organization (UNIDO) 13

International Conference on Financing for Development (Monterrey Conference) 67, 68

International Monetary Fund (IMF) 68, 71

Millennium Summit 10

Official Development Assistance (ODA) 67

Special Fund 53

water 63

weapons of mass destruction 39

World Bank, the 17, 63, 67, 71-72

World Commission on Environment and Development (Rio Earth Summit) 39, 41, 44

World Summit on Sustainable Development (WSSD) 41, 47

World Trade Organization (WTO) 71–72, 75

World War II 17, 67, 72

Picture Credits

Benjamin Stewart: pp. 48, 50
Corbis: p. 64
Corel: pp. 52, 56, 57
Corel (United Nations): pp. 14, 34, 37, 55, 59, 62
iStock: pp. 45, 71
    Amanda Rohde: p. 18
    Anastasios Kandris: p. 49
    Constantin Simian: p. 12
    Dustin Stellar: p. 15
    Feily Matias: p. 66
    Justin Long: p. 60
    Mark Stay: p. 20
    Mike Lindberg: p. 23
    Natalia Bratslavsky: p. 9
    Piotrek Golebiowski: p. 69
    Roman Levin: p. 16
Jupiter Images: pp. 24, 25, 27, 28, 30, 33, 38, 40, 42, 70, 73, 74
National Park Service: p. 46
PhotoSpin: p. 10

To the best knowledge of the publisher, all other images are in the public domain. If any image has been inadvertently uncredited, please notify Harding House Publishing Service, Vestal, New York 13850, so that rectification can be made for future printings.

Biographies

Author

Heather Docalavich first became interested in the work of the United Nations while working as an adviser for a high school Model UN program. She lives in Hilton Head Island, South Carolina, with her four children.

Series Consultant

Bruce Russett is Dean Acheson Professor of Political Science at Yale University and editor of the *Journal of Conflict Resolution*. He has taught or researched at Columbia, Harvard, M.I.T., Michigan, and North Carolina in the United States, and educational institutions in Belgium, Britain, Israel, Japan, and the Netherlands. He has been president of the International Studies Association and the Peace Science Society, holds an honorary doctorate from Uppsala University in Sweden. He was principal adviser to the U.S. Catholic Bishops for their pastoral letter on nuclear deterrence in 1985, and co-directed the staff for the 1995 Ford Foundation Report, *The United Nations in Its Second Half Century.* He has served as editor of the *Journal of Conflict Resolution* since 1973. The twenty-five books he has published include *The Once and Future Security Council* (1997), *Triangulating Peace: Democracy, Interdependence, and International Organizations* (2001), *World Politics: The Menu for Choice* (8th edition 2006), and *Purpose and Policy in the Global Community* (2006).